AAT

Indirect Tax
Finance Act 2020

For assessments from 1 January 2021 to 31 January 2022

Pocket notes

These Pocket Notes support study for the following AAT qualifications:

AAT Advanced Diploma in Accounting - Level 3

AAT Advanced Certificate in Bookkeeping - Level 3

AAT Advanced Diploma in Accounting at SCQF - Level 6

British library cataloguing-in-publication data

A catalogue record for this book is available from the British Library.

Published by:
Kaplan Publishing UK
Unit 2 The Business Centre
Molly Millars Lane
Wokingham
Berkshire
RG41 2QZ

ISBN 978-1-78740-820-3

© Kaplan Financial Limited, 2020

Printed and bound in Great Britain.

CONTENTS

Preface

These Pocket Notes contain the key things that you need to know for the assessment, presented in a unique visual way that makes revision easy and effective.

Written by experienced lecturers and authors, these Pocket Notes break down content into manageable chunks to maximise your concentration.

Quality and accuracy are of the utmost importance to us so if you spot an error in any of our products, please send an email to mykaplanreporting@kaplan.com with full details, or follow the link to the feedback form in MyKaplan.

Our Quality Co-ordinator will work with our technical team to verify the error and take action to ensure it is corrected in future editions.

A guide to the assessment

- AAT indirect tax reference material.
- The keys to success in AAT indirect tax.

The assessment

IDRX is the indirect taxation unit studied on the Advanced Diploma in Accounting qualification.

Indirect tax is assessed by means of a computer based assessment. The CBA will last for 90 minutes and consists of 8 tasks.

In any one assessment, students may not be assessed on all content, or on the full depth or breadth of a piece of content.

The content assessed may change over time to ensure validity of assessment, but all assessment criteria will be tested over time.

Learning outcomes & weighting

1.	Understand and apply VAT legislation requirements	30%
2.	Accurately complete VAT returns and submit them in a timely manner	40%
3.	Understand the implications for the business of errors, omissions and late filing and payment	20%
4.	Report VAT-related information within the organisation in accordance with regulatory and organisational requirement	10%
	Total	100%

Pass mark

To pass a unit assessment, students need to achieve a mark of 70% or more.

This unit contributes 10% of the total amount required for the Advanced Diploma in Accounting qualification.

Format of objective test questions

The standard task formats that will be used for any computer based assessment are as follows:

- True or False (tick boxes).
- Multiple choice, with anything from three to six options available.
- Gap fill, using either words or numbers.
- Pick lists, or drop down options, which are quite likely for tax returns.
- Drag and drop, which can only be used if the question and the possible answers can fit on one screen.
- Hybrids, a mixture of the above.

AAT indirect tax reference material

In your assessment a large amount of reference material can be accessed by clicking on the appropriate link on the right hand side of the screen.

It is essential that you are familiar with this material provided, as it will save you having to memorise a large amount of information.

Throughout these notes we have indicated areas where it will be particularly useful for you to look at your reference material.

The reference material is included at the back of the Kaplan study text. It can also be downloaded from the AAT website.

The keys to success in AAT indirect tax

- Attempt all of the tasks in the assessment.
- Practise questions to improve your ability to apply the techniques and perform the calculations.
- When completing the VAT return in the assessment ensure figures are entered in the correct boxes.
- Follow any instructions given about entering numbers to the nearest penny or nearest pound.
- If no special instructions are given then enter numbers in Boxes 1 to 5 of the VAT return in pounds and pence (e.g. £4,000.00 not £4,000) and in boxes 6 to 9 to the nearest £.

1

Introduction to VAT

- VAT – how it works.
- Overview of VAT.
- Types of supply.
- Recovery of input VAT.
- Output VAT.
- Partial exemption.
- Sources of information.
- Keeping up-to-date with VAT.
- HMRC powers.
- Disputes with HMRC.
- Visits by VAT officers.
- Contacting HMRC.

VAT – how it works

VAT is:

- an indirect tax on consumer spending
- charged on most goods and services supplied within the UK
- suffered by the final consumer, and
- collected by businesses on behalf of HMRC at each stage in the production and distribution process.

Businesses do not suffer any tax.

The final unregistered end consumer who cannot recover the input VAT that suffers the tax.

Illustration (assuming the rate of VAT is 20% throughout)

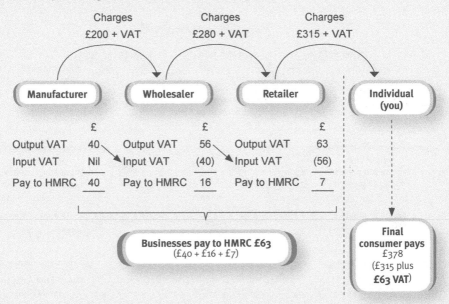

	Charges £200 + VAT	Charges £280 + VAT	Charges £315 + VAT

Manufacturer → **Wholesaler** → **Retailer** → **Individual (you)**

	£		£		£
Output VAT	40	Output VAT	56	Output VAT	63
Input VAT	Nil	Input VAT	(40)	Input VAT	(56)
Pay to HMRC	40	Pay to HMRC	16	Pay to HMRC	7

Businesses pay to HMRC £63
(£40 + £16 + £7)

Final consumer pays
£378
(£315 plus
£63 VAT)

Overview of VAT

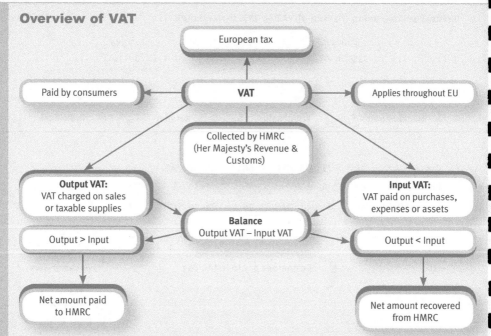

Types of supply

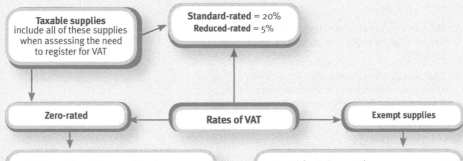

Taxable supplies
include all of these supplies when assessing the need to register for VAT

Standard-rated = 20%
Reduced-rated = 5%

Zero-rated

Rates of VAT

Exempt supplies

- Water and most types of food.
- Books and newspapers.
- Drugs and medicines.
- Public transport.
- Children's clothing and footwear.
- Sewerage and water services.
- New house building.

- Land (including rent).
- Insurance.
- Postal services.
- Betting, gaming and lotteries.
- Finance.
- Non-profit making education.
- Health services (doctors and dentists).

CBA focus

You need to be aware of the different rates of VAT that apply.

However, no knowledge is required of the details of which specific items fall into each category.

The indirect tax reference material provided in the assessment gives the different rates of VAT in the 'Rates of VAT' section.

Types of supply: impact

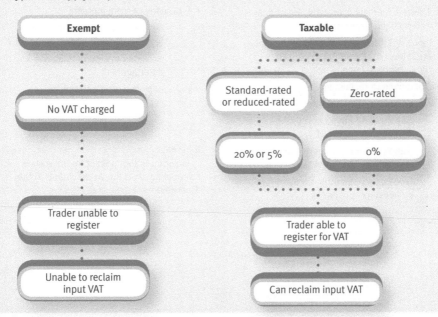

KAPLAN PUBLISHING

Recovery of input VAT

- There is no distinction between capital and revenue expenditure.
- Input VAT can be recovered on capital purchases and revenue expenses, provided conditions satisfied.
- Conditions to reclaim input VAT:
  - Must be registered trader.
  - Supply must have been to the person making the claim.
  - Supply must be properly supported, normally by VAT invoice.
  - Goods/services must be used for business purposes.

Irrecoverable (blocked) VAT

- Business entertainment
  - includes hospitality of any kind (e.g. food, drink, accommodation)
  - excludes overseas business entertainment
  - excludes staff entertainment.

CBA focus

Information about entertainment expenses is included in the indirect tax reference material given in the assessment, in the 'Entertainment expenses' section.

- Motor cars
  - Purchase – only recoverable if used 100% for business (e.g. taxi, driving school car).
  - Motor expenses – provided some business use then 100% recoverable.
- Fuel – several situations are possible
  - only use fuel for business purposes and reclaim all input tax
  - reclaim VAT on all fuel including for private use and pay appropriate fuel scale charge
  - If claiming the scale charge the VAT element of the scale charge is added to output tax, then the VAT element of all fuel (business and private) is added to input tax.
  - only claim input VAT on fuel for business use, needs detailed records
  - don't reclaim any input VAT (on any vehicles).

CBA focus

The indirect tax reference material given in the assessment contains full details on cars and motoring expenses in the 'Vehicles and motoring expenses' section.

Output VAT

- Registered traders must charge output tax on all taxable supplies at the appropriate rate.
- This includes sales of capital assets.

Sales of capital assets

- VAT normally charged at the standard rate on the sale price.
- Cars:
  - if input tax on purchase was irrecoverable (blocked): treat as exempt sale
  - If input VAT on purchase was recoverable: add output VAT on sale price.

Partial exemption

Traders who make both taxable and exempt supplies are given credit for only part of the input tax they incur.

This section deals with the calculation of the recoverable input tax credit.

Methods of determining recoverable input tax

The standard method for determining the amount of recoverable input VAT is as follows:

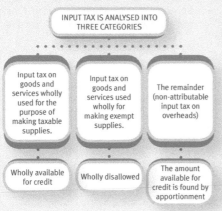

INPUT TAX IS ANALYSED INTO THREE CATEGORIES

Input tax on goods and services wholly used for the purpose of making taxable supplies.	Input tax on goods and services used wholly for making exempt supplies.	The remainder (non-attributable input tax on overheads)
Wholly available for credit	Wholly disallowed	The amount available for credit is found by apportionment

- If input tax wholly or partly attributed to exempt supplies is below a de minimis limit, all input tax is available for credit.

CBA focus

The indirect tax reference material given in the assessment provides some information about partial exemption in the 'Exempt and partly-exempt business' section.

Sources of information

CBA focus

The indirect tax reference material given in the assessment contains some information about sources of information in the 'Finding out more information about VAT' section.

Legislation

- The main source of law on VAT is the VAT Act 1994 as amended by annual Finance Acts and other regulations issued by Parliament.

HMRC website

VAT Guide

- HMRC booklet: VAT Guide (VAT Notice 700) is the main guide to VAT rules and procedures.

VAT notes and announcements

- Quarterly bulletin sent to all registered traders. Gives news of all changes and helps keep traders up-to-date. Latest news published on HMRC homepage - businesses can receive email alerts.

VAT enquiries helpline

Available if HMRC website does not have an answer to your query.

Keeping up-to-date with VAT

VAT rules change frequently and it is important to keep up-to-date.

- Stops business misclassifying supplies
- Stops the business charging the wrong rate of VAT
- Helps prevent penalties for incorrect returns
- Ensures changes are actioned on the correct date
- Keeping up-to-date is essential to demonstrate professional competence and due care as required by the AAT Code of Professional Ethics.

Methods of keeping up-to-date

- HMRC website at www.hmrc.gov.uk
- Detailed VAT rules at www.gov.uk/topic/business-tax/vat
- Circulars from accountancy firms
- Specialist tax journals
- Relevant CPD (continuing professional development) courses

HMRC powers

HMRC is the government department responsible for administering tax in the United Kingdom.

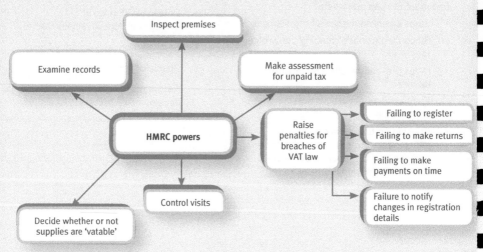

Disputes with HMRC

- Taxpayer has choice of:
  - Review of case by another HMRC officer and/or
  - Appeal to the tax tribunal (usually first tier).
- If taxpayer dissatisfied with review they can still appeal to the Tribunal.

Visits by VAT officers

VAT officers can make control visits to registered traders to check records and ensure VAT is being calculated correctly.

Contacting HMRC

If taxpayers have VAT queries they should take one or more of the following actions in the order listed below.

(1) Research HMRC website.

(2) Contact the VAT helpline.

(3) Write to HMRC, preferably by email.

Note that HMRC advise that taxpayers get rulings on contentious areas in writing.

CBA focus

More information about communicating with HMRC can be found in the indirect tax reference material in the 'Finding out more information about VAT' section.

VAT registration

- Registration for VAT.
- Compulsory registration.
- Consequences of registration.
- Voluntary registration.
- Deregistration.
- Record keeping.

Registration for VAT

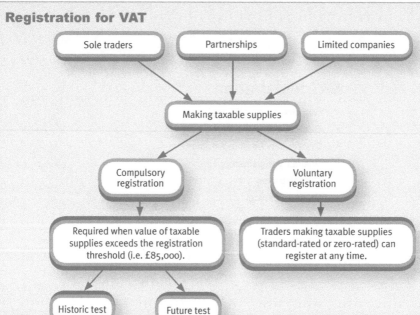

Compulsory registration

Historic turnover test	Future test
• Taxable supplies in the last 12 months exceed £85,000.	• Taxable supplies in the next 30 days in isolation are likely to exceed £85,000.
• Perform test at the end of each month.	• Perform test constantly.
Inform HMRC:	
• within 30 days of the end of the month in which the threshold is exceeded.	• By the end of the 30 day period in which the threshold is expected to be exceeded.
Registered from:	
• the first day of the second month after taxable supplies exceeded the threshold, or	• From the start of the 30 day period.
• an agreed earlier date.	

- Note that taxable supplies for registration purposes:

  - Includes standard, reduced and zero-rated supplies.

  - Excludes sale of capital assets.

More than one business

- Person, not business, required to register.
- Person = individual, partnership or company.
- Single registration required for an individual.
  - Covers all sole trader businesses
  - Turnover of all sole trader businesses owned by one person should be considered together (e.g. if taxable supplies in all businesses together > £85,000 then the person must register for VAT).
- A separate registration is required for a company, even if its main shareholder already has a VAT registration themselves.

Exemption from registration

- Can apply for exemption if make only zero-rated supplies.
- Then unable to reclaim input VAT.
- Avoids administrative burden of complying with VAT regulations.

Consequences of registration

Accounting for VAT

- Must start accounting for VAT.
- Output tax must be charged on taxable supplies.
- Given VAT registration number which must be quoted on all invoices.
- Will be allocated a tax period for filing returns, normally every three months.
- Can recover input tax on most business purchases and expenses (except irrecoverable amounts – see Chapter 1). This can also include certain input VAT incurred before registration.
- Appropriate VAT records must be kept (see below).
- Receive certificate of registration which contains registration number and is proof of registration.

Failure to register

If a trader fails to register when over the compulsory registration threshold:

- All VAT the trader should have charged from the date they should have registered is payable to HMRC. The trader will have to pay this VAT out of their own profits.
- A penalty can be charged based on a percentage of the VAT due.

CBA focus

The indirect tax reference material given in the assessment covers the registration thresholds and rules for registration in the 'Registration and deregistration thresholds' section.

Voluntary registration

Advantages	Disadvantages
• Input tax recoverable.	• Output tax charged on sales:
• If making zero-rated supplies VAT returns will show VAT repayable. Can register for monthly returns to aid cashflow.	– if make standard or reduced-rated supplies to customers who are not VAT registered, will be an additional cost to them
• Avoids penalties for late registration.	– may affect competitiveness.
• May give the impression of a more substantial business.	• VAT administration.

CBA focus

The advantages and disadvantages of voluntary registration are given in the indirect tax reference material provided in the assessment, in the 'Registration and deregistration limits' section.

KAPLAN PUBLISHING

Deregistration

Compulsory deregistration	Voluntary deregistration
• When cease to make taxable supplies. Inform HMRC: • Within 30 days of ceasing to make taxable supplies. Deregistered from: • Date of cessation.	• If value of expected taxable supplies in the next 12 months will not be > £83,000. • At any time when above test satisfied. • Date of request for deregistration, or • An agreed later date.

Consequences of deregistration

• Output VAT must be paid on the value of business assets held at date when cease to be a taxable person (e.g. capital items, trading stock/inventory).

CBA focus

Registration and deregistration are always popular exam topics.

Record keeping

General requirements

Generally, businesses must keep records of:

- All taxable and exempt supplies made in the course of business.
- All taxable supplies received in the course of business.
- A summary of the total output tax and input tax for each tax period

    = the VAT account (see Chapter 6).

Failure to keep records can lead to a penalty.

Retention of records

- Must retain records for **6 years**
    - HMRC may reduce the time period if records bulky
    - may be stored electronically.

Details to be kept.

- Type of records to retain:
    - orders and delivery notes
    - relevant business correspondence
    - appointment and job books
    - purchases and sales day books
    - cash books and other account books
    - bank statements, paying-in slips and cheque stubs
    - purchase invoices and copy sales invoices
    - records of daily takings, including till rolls
    - annual accounts
    - import and export documents
    - VAT accounts
    - any credit notes issued or received.

CBA focus

Businesses do not need to keep records of estimates or pro-forma invoices.

CBA focus

You should be able to list the records that must be kept for VAT.

Much of this detail on record keeping and lists of records required is included in the indirect tax reference material given in the assessment. It can be found in the 'Keeping business and VAT records' section.

Electronic and paper VAT records

- Records can be kept in whatever format that the business prefers (paper and/or electronic).
- Records must be easily accessible if a VAT officer visits.
- Records can be kept on microfilm provided HMRC have given approval and the records can be inspected when necessary.
- Some businesses send or receive invoices by electronic means (e.g. email). This does not require approval from HMRC.

Control visits

- Registered businesses may be visited by a VAT officer on occasion to ensure that their records are being correctly maintained.

3

VAT documentation

- VAT invoices.
- Discounts.
- Tax point.
- Other documentation.
- Changes in VAT legislation.

VAT invoices

Full VAT invoice

- Must issue a VAT invoice within 30 days of the earlier date:
  - date of the supply, or
  - receipt of payment.
- VAT invoices do not have to be issued if:
  - Supplies are wholly zero-rated or exempt.
  - Customer is not VAT-registered.
- Invoices are regarded as issued when they are sent or given to a customer.

Simplified (less detailed) VAT invoice

- A simplified tax invoice may be issued if the VAT-inclusive supply value does not exceed £250.

Retention of invoices

All businesses must keep records of:

- all sales invoices issued except
  - copies of simplified VAT invoices need not be kept.
- all purchase invoices for items purchased for business purposes except those
  - with a gross value of ≤ £25, and
  - purchased from a coin operated telephone, or vending machine, or for car parking charges or tolls.

Full VAT invoices must show:

- Identifying number
- Date of issue of invoice
- Date of supply (tax point) if different from invoice date*
- Supplier's name and address*
- Supplier's VAT registration number*
- Name and address of customer
- Type of supply (e.g. sale, hire purchase)*
- Description/quantity of goods/services*
- Unit price or rate, excluding VAT
- Rate of tax and amount payable excluding VAT for each item
- Total amount payable (excluding VAT)
- Prompt payment discount offered
- Rate and amount of VAT charged for each rate of VAT
- Total amount of VAT chargeable.

Note that you do not need to include information such as:

- Order number or order date
- Customer's VAT registration number
- Method of delivery.

Items marked with an asterisk are required on a simplified invoice (see below).

Simplified (less detailed) invoices

Less detailed VAT invoice must show:

- the items marked with an asterisk, plus:
- the amount payable (including VAT) for each rate (standard and zero)

Note that there is no need to show the amount of VAT charged – it is sufficient that it is included in the invoice total.

- You do not need to keep copies of simplified invoices.

E-invoicing

- Invoices can be in electronic form
- Must be a secure format like a pdf.

CBA focus

Full details of the contents of invoices are included in the indirect tax reference material provided in the assessment in the 'VAT invoices' section.

Calculation of VAT at standard rate

- If given VAT-exclusive (net) amounts:
  - VAT = (Net amount x 20/100).
- If given VAT-inclusive (gross) amounts:
  - VAT = (Gross amount x 20/120) (or 1/6).
  - Net amount = (Gross amount x 100/120) (or 5/6).

Other rates of VAT

- If given VAT-exclusive (net) amounts:

$$\text{VAT} = \text{Net amount} \times \frac{\text{VAT rate}}{100}$$

- If given VAT-inclusive (gross) amounts:

$$\text{VAT} = \text{Gross amount} \times \frac{\text{VAT rate}}{100 + \text{VAT rate}}$$

Net amount

$$= \text{Gross amount} \times \frac{100}{100 + \text{VAT rate}}$$

Discounts

- **Trade discounts** and **bulk buy discounts**
  = deducted before VAT is calculated.
- If a business offers to pay a customer's VAT the amount paid by the customer
  = treated as the VAT-inclusive amount.

Prompt payment discounts

- VAT must be calculated on the price the customer actually pays.
- A customer may or may not be eligible for the prompt payment discount so the amount paid is not certain in advance.
- Methods of dealing with this:
  - invoice the full amount with subsequent credit note if customer receives discount
  - invoice the discounted amount with subsequent further invoice if customer does not take discount
  - invoice full amount but show on the invoice the effect of the discount and VAT so that the customer knows the correct figure of input tax to claim if they take discount.

Rounding

- Total VAT payable on an invoice should be rounded down to the nearest penny in the assessment.
- Any fraction of a penny is ignored.

CBA focus

Treatment of discounts is covered in the indirect tax reference material provided in the assessment in the 'VAT invoices' section.

Tax point

- Tax point = time of supply.
- Determines:
  - the VAT return period in which the supply is accounted for
  - the rate of VAT (where there is a change in rate or a change in the classification of a supply).

Basic tax point

Goods =
Date goods are made available (i.e. delivery or customer takes away)

Services =
Date services are performed/completed

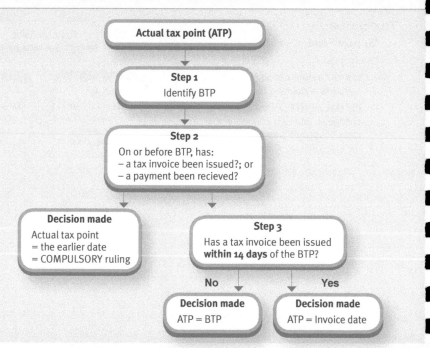

14 day rule

Note that the 14 day rule:

- can be extended (with agreement from HMRC) to accommodate month end invoicing systems.
- only applies to tax invoices.
- does not apply to invoices which are wholly for zero-rated goods (e.g. exports).

CBA focus

Always apply the 14 day rule unless the task in the assessment suggests an extension has been agreed with HMRC.

Deposits

- Any deposits received in advance create a tax point which is the earlier of:
  - Date of issue of VAT invoice requesting deposit
  - Date deposit is received.
- VAT element of deposit must be calculated and accounted for.
- No tax point created for returnable deposit.

Goods on sale or return

The basic tax point is the earliest of the:

- date the goods are adopted (accepted by customer)
- date payment is received (except for refundable deposits)
- expiration of the time limit for adopting the goods, or
- 12 months from the date the goods were despatched.

Continuous supplies

If services are performed on a continuous basis with payments received regularly or from time to time, there is a tax point every time, which is the earlier of the date:

- a VAT invoice is issued, or
- a payment is received.

Where regular payments received, supplier can send one invoice at start of period (usually a year) to cover all payments due in that period.

In this case the supplying business accounts for output VAT on the earlier of the:

- payment date for each regular payment, or
- date payment received.

The customer can reclaim input VAT at the same time.

Other documentation

Credit and debit notes

- Credit notes are issued by suppliers to cancel out part of an original sales invoice.

- Alternatively they can wait for their customer to issue them with a debit note. Debit notes are issued by a customer to cancel out part of an original purchase invoice.

- Suppliers and customers can only account for one of these – either both account for the suppliers credit note or both account for the customer's debit note.

- Credit or debit notes should contain similar information to the original invoice plus the reason for the credit request.

A supplier is not allowed to issue a credit note to recover VAT on bad debts.

If the supplier issues the credit note without making a VAT adjustment, the note must say **'This is not a credit note for VAT'**.

Effect of credit or debit notes

	SELLER (supplier)	BUYER (customer)
Seller issues credit note	Deduct from output tax	Deduct from input tax
Buyer issues debit note	Deduct from output tax	Deduct from input tax
Overall effect	Reduces VAT payable	Increases VAT payable

Pro-forma invoices

When supplier issues invoice to customer, VAT payable to HMRC
when VAT return next submitted.

What if customer has not paid invoice?

Supplier still liable for VAT element of sales invoice.

Businesses therefore unlikely to issue a tax invoice before goods despatched.

Business may issue a pro-forma invoice
= an offer to supply goods or services and a request for payment.
– does not rank as a VAT invoice.

Pro-forma invoices should be clearly marked **'This is not a VAT invoice'**.
– supplier not required to pay VAT.

Once the customer accepts the goods or services offered, and/or payment received,
supplier issues "live" VAT invoice to replace pro-forma.

Statements and demands for payment

- Only VAT invoices and credit and debit notes should be entered in the VAT records.
- Demand for payment or a statement has no VAT implication as VAT has already been recorded.

Orders and delivery notes

- Ignored for VAT.
- Cannot be used by a customer as evidence for reclaiming VAT on their purchases.

VAT-only invoices

- May be issued to increase VAT charged on an earlier invoice/ if forgot to include VAT.
- Entered in the VAT records and the tax paid over to HMRC as usual.
- Purchaser will be able to recover the VAT charged.

CBA focus

Information about credit notes, debit notes and pro-forma invoices is included in the indirect tax reference material provided in the assessment, in the 'VAT invoices' section.

Changes in VAT legislation

Change in the rate of VAT

- Tax point date = very important:
  - when there is a change in the rate of VAT, or
  - if a supply is reclassified from one rate of VAT to another.

Effect of a VAT rate change on a business

Generally:

- Sales invoices need to use correct rate of VAT.
- Sales prices used in quotes/pricing invoices must include correct rate of VAT.
- Prices displayed to the public must be correct.
- Staff expense claims must reclaim correct rate of VAT.
- Input VAT reclaimed for purchases and expenses should be the figure shown on the invoice.
- Business may choose to maintain current prices and absorb the VAT increase/ decrease in their profits.

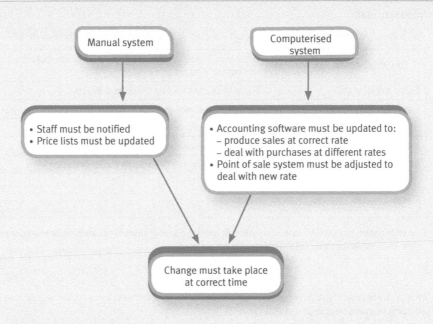

Informing staff

The following staff within a business would need to be told about a rate change and its effects:

IT department staff	To ensure relevant changes are made to computerised accounting system
Sales ledger staff	To raise or check sales invoices correctly
Purchase ledger staff	So they can check purchase invoices correctly
Sales staff	To ensure customers are given correct prices
Marketing department staff	So any new brochures or publicity material is correct
Staff generally	To ensure expense claims are made correctly

CBA focus

Full information about VAT documentation is included in the indirect tax reference material provided in the assessment in the 'VAT documentation' section.

CBA focus

In your assessment you may have to communicate VAT information by completing a simple email advising relevant people of the change.

4

VAT accounting schemes

- Normal scheme.
- Annual accounting scheme.
- Cash accounting scheme.
- Flat rate scheme.

Normal scheme

Return period
- Usually quarterly
- Elect for monthly returns if receive repayments.

Known as VAT 100 form
(See Chapter 6)

VAT return
Summarises transactions
for VAT return period

Submission dates
- Return due within 1 month and 7 days of end of return period
- All businesses, with very few exceptions, must file online.

Payment of VAT
- Electronic payments:
  - must be made if returns submitted online
  - may be made when paper returns are submitted
  - payment date within 1 month and 7 days of end of return period
  - direct debit payments get further 3 working days after the 7 day period.

Making tax digital

- Applies to most VAT registered businesses with taxable turnover in excess of the VAT registration threshold.

- Such businesses are required to keep digital records and to submit VAT returns using MTD-compatible software.

- VAT registered businesses with taxable turnover below the registration threshold can choose to adopt the scheme if they want to.

- A soft landing period applies until 1 April 2021 for a business to be able to establish the necessary digital links. This permits the use of functions such as "copy and paste" to achieve the transfer of data until this period expires.

Payments of VAT

Online payments are normally made 7 days after the one month deadline.

Note that HMRC require payments to clear their bank account by this date.

This extra 7 days does not apply if the trader:

- uses the annual accounting scheme, or
- has to make monthly payments (compulsory for large businesses).

If paid by direct debit the payment is taken from the business account three working days after the 7 day period allowed for electronic payments.

Other electronic payment methods include:

- By debit or credit card over the internet
- Telephone banking payments
- BACS direct credit
- Bank Giro.

Repayments of VAT

- If Box 4 is larger than Box 3 then a repayment of VAT is due.
- HMRC make additional checks on the return to ensure the claim is valid.
- Repayments are made directly into the trader's bank account – usually within 10 working days of receiving the return.
- Traders who regularly receive repayments can choose to submit monthly returns.
- No automatic refund if there is an outstanding debt due to HMRC.

CBA focus

Information about making tax digital, and submission and payment dates is included in the indirect tax reference material provided in the assessment in the 'VAT periods, submitting returns and paying VAT' section.

Annual accounting scheme

Operation	Conditions

• One VAT return prepared a year.
• Return due:
  – 2 months after end of annual VAT period.
• Payments on account (POA):
  – 9 POA due end of months 4–12
  – Each POA is 10% of VAT for previous year.
• New businesses base POA on estimated VAT liability.
• Balancing payment/repayment due with VAT return.
• All payments made electronically (but no extra 7 day rule).
	• To join must expect taxable turnover <=£1,350,000 for the next 12 months (excluding VAT and sale of capital assets).
	• VAT payments and returns must be up-to-date.
	• Must leave if taxable turnover in next 12 months will be > £1,600,000.
	
	If a business takes over another, the estimated combined taxable turnover in the next 12 months is compared to £1,600,000.

Advantages	Disadvantages

• Reduces administration.
• Regular payments can help cashflow.
	• Not useful if:
	  – in repayment position.
	  – Taxable turnover decreasing (interim payments higher than under normal scheme).

Key point

The annual accounting scheme can be used with cash accounting scheme or flat rate scheme, but not both.

CBA focus

Information about all three VAT accounting schemes is included in the indirect tax reference material provided in the assessment in the 'Special accounting schemes' section.

Cash accounting scheme

Operation	Conditions
• VAT accounted for on cash payments and cash receipts. • Must be recorded separately in cash book.	• To join must expect taxable turnover <=£1,350,000 for the next 12 months (excluding VAT and sale of capital assets). • VAT payments and returns must be up to date. • No convictions for VAT offences/penalties for dishonest conduct. • Must leave if taxable turnover > £1,600,000 If a business takes over another, the estimated combined taxable turnover in the next 12 months is compared to £1,600,000.

Advantages	Disadvantages
• Do not pay output tax until receive payment from customer. • Provides automatic relief for irrecoverable/ bad debts. • Can be used with annual accounting.	• Delays recovery of input VAT. Not useful if: • Making zero-rated supplies • Making lots of cash sales.

Flat rate scheme

Operation	Conditions

• Flat rate of VAT applied to total turnover (including exempt supplies and VAT).
 	
 • No input VAT recovered.
 	
 • Flat rate determined by trade sector.
 	
 • Flat rate only used to simplify preparation of VAT return
   – still need to issue tax invoices
   – must still maintain VAT account.
 	
 • If a business qualifies as a limited cost business then VAT will be calculated using a rate of 16.5%.
	• To join must expect taxable turnover <=£150,000 for the next 12 months (excluding VAT).
	
	 • Businesses are eligible to stay in the scheme until their VAT-inclusive income (i.e. all turnover including taxable and exempt supplies) for the previous 12 months exceeds £230,000.
	
	 If a business takes over another, the estimated combined taxable turnover in the next 12 months is compared to £230,000.

Advantages	Disadvantages
• Reduces administration.	• Flat rate percentage based on average sales mix for trade sector.
• Do not have to decide whether input VAT recoverable.	• Not suitable if have higher proportion of zero-rated/exempt supplies than trade sector.
• Do not need to account for VAT on individual purchases.	
• Discount of 1% in first year of registration.	• Not suitable for businesses often in repayment position.
• May reduce total VAT payable.	• Not suitable if have higher proportion of standard-rated purchases than trade sector.
• Business has certainty, as percentage of turnover payable as VAT known in advance.	
• Less chance of errors in calculating VAT.	
• Can be used with annual accounting scheme.	

CBA focus

All of the accounting schemes are covered in the indirect tax reference material provided in the assessment, including details of the advantages and disadvantages. These can be found in the 'Special accounting schemes' section.

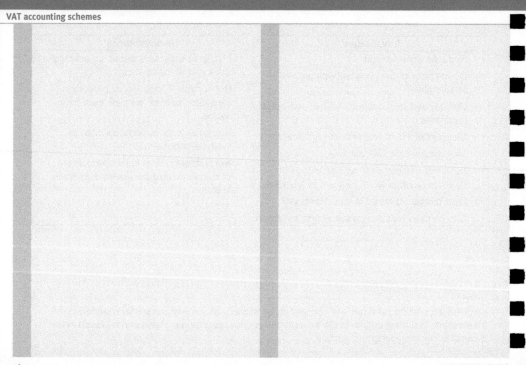

5

VAT errors and penalties

- Ethical considerations.
- VAT evasion and avoidance.
- VAT penalties.
- Errors on VAT returns.
- Default surcharge.

Ethical considerations

AAT members and students are required to follow the AAT Code of Professional Ethics.

These require that AAT members act with:

- integrity
- objectivity
- professional competence and due care
- confidentiality
- professional behaviour.

Members must

- comply with relevant laws
- avoid actions that discredit the profession
- ensure information given to HMRC is accurate and complete.

Members must not:

- assist clients to plan or commit an offence.

VAT evasion and avoidance

Evasion – illegal ways of reducing VAT liability.

Avoidance – legal ways to reduce VAT liability.

Any deliberate attempt to evade tax would be a breach of integrity and professional behaviour and must be resisted.

VAT penalties

Error/omissions	Action
Failing to register	HMRC can issue assessment to collect tax due and charge a penalty.
Failure to submit a return	HMRC can issue an assessment to collect tax due.
Failure to tell HMRC that an assessment is too low within 30 days	Penalty can be charged.
Making a non-careless error	Trader must take steps to correct otherwise error may be regarded as careless.
Making a careless or deliberate error	Inclusion on Form VAT 652 or by letter. If careless and below limit can include on next return. A penalty can be charged.

Error/omissions	Action
Errors found by HMRC	HMRC can raise an assessment within 4 years of the end of the VAT period (careless errors) or 20 years (deliberate errors like fraud). A penalty can be charged.
Submitting VAT return late or paying late (see below)	Default surcharge regime applies.
Failure disclose business changes	Penalty can be charged.

CBA focus

Details of penalties are covered in the indirect tax reference material provided in the assessment in the 'Surcharges, penalties and assessment' section.

Errors on VAT returns

```
┌─────────────────────────────┐        ┌─────────────────────────────┐
│ FOUND BY TRADER AND         │        │ FOUND BY HMRC               │
│ DISCLOSED VOLUNTARILY       │        │                             │
└─────────────────────────────┘        └─────────────────────────────┘
```

```
┌─────────────────────────────────────┐        ┌─────────────────────────────────────┐
│ De minimis threshold of error =      │        │ Issue assessment within 4 years of  │
│ greater of                           │        │ relevant VAT period (increase to 20  │
│ (i)  £10,000, and                    │        │ years if deliberate error)          │
│ (ii) 1% of turnover, subject to an   │        └─────────────────────────────────────┘
│      upper limit of £50,000          │
└─────────────────────────────────────┘
```

```
┌──────────────────────────┐        ┌─────────────────────────────────────────┐
│ Net error                │        │ Net error > de minimis threshold or is  │
│ ≤ de minimis threshold:  │        │ deliberate or relates to an accounting  │
│ and not deliberate:      │        │ period that ended > 4 years ago: –      │
│ – Include on next VAT    │        │ Separate notification on Form VAT 652   │
│   return or disclose     │        │ or by letter                            │
│   separately             │        └─────────────────────────────────────────┘
└──────────────────────────┘
```

```
┌─────────────────────────────┐
│ Standard penalty            │
└─────────────────────────────┘
```

Separate disclosure of errors

Information that should be provided to HMRC if the error is not corrected on the next return:

- how the error happened
- the amount of the error
- the VAT period in which it occurred
- whether the error was involving input or output tax
- how you worked out the error
- whether the error is in favour of the business or HMRC.

Note that a taxpayer must use Form VAT 652 (or a letter) for larger errors but may use the form for smaller errors if desired.

CBA focus

Correction of errors is an important topic.

Error limits and correction are dealt with in the indirect tax reference material, provided in the assessment in the 'Errors in previous VAT returns' section.

Default surcharge

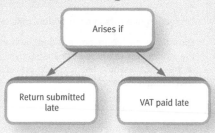

Arises if

Return submitted late

VAT paid late

Reasonable excuse

- If reasonable excuse then no surcharge liability notice issued.
- Examples:
    - Computer breakdown
    - Fire or flood
    - Illness of key employee
    - Sudden cash crisis.

CBA focus

Some information about surcharges is included in the indirect tax reference material provided in the assessment in the 'Surcharges, penalties and assessment' section.

Consequences

First default	• HMRC serve a surcharge liability notice.
	• Specifies a surcharge period:
	– Ending 12 months after the end of the VAT period to which the default relates.
Further defaults	• Surcharge period extended to:
	– 12 months after the end of the VAT period to which the latest default relates.
	• If default involves late payment of VAT
	– surcharge penalty levied.

VAT returns

- The VAT return.
- Place of supply.
- Imports and exports of goods.
- Supplies of services.
- Completing the VAT return.
- Relief for irrecoverable/ bad debts.

The VAT return

VAT return
Summarises transactions for VAT return period

Return period
- Usually quarterly
- Elect for monthly returns if receive repayments

Known as VAT 100 form

CBA focus

In your assessment you will be required to complete a VAT return.

Guidance on completing the VAT return is included in the indirect tax reference material provided in the assessment in the 'Completing the VAT return, box by box' section.

Place of supply

The place of supply rules help to decide how VAT is charged.

In broad terms the rules are as follows:

Goods

These are treated as supplied in the country where the goods originate.

Services

(a) Business to business (B2B) (i.e. supplies to business customers).

The supply is treated as made in the country where the **customer** is based.

If the customer is based in the EU then VAT must be applied by the customer following the 'reverse charge' procedure.

(b) Business to customer (B2C) (i.e. supplies to non-business customers (e.g. individuals) and unregistered businesses).

The supply is treated as made in the country where the **supplier** is located.

Therefore, if the supplier is based in the EU then VAT must be applied in the normal way.

Imports and exports of goods

Exports and imports to/from non-EU members

Exports
Goods exported: normally treated as zero-rated.
Include sales in Box 6.

← **Non-EU members** →

Imports
Goods imported from outside the EU may be subject to VAT and customs duty when they enter the country.

↓

Goods taxed at standard rate if supplied in UK?

Yes

- Subject to VAT.
- Subject to customs duty.
- VAT reclaimed as input VAT.
- Include VAT in Box 4.
- Include purchases in Box 7.

No

- Not subject to VAT.
- Subject to customs duty.

Exports and imports to/from countries within the EU

Movements of goods between EU member states known as acquisitions (for the buyer) and despatches (for the seller).

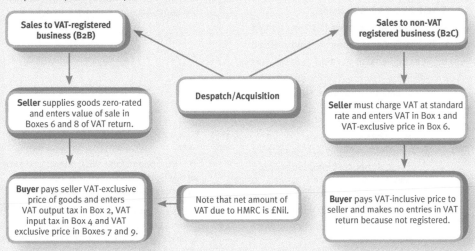

Sales to VAT-registered business (B2B)

Despatch/Acquisition

Sales to non-VAT registered business (B2C)

Seller supplies goods zero-rated and enters value of sale in Boxes 6 and 8 of VAT return.

Seller must charge VAT at standard rate and enters VAT in Box 1 and VAT-exclusive price in Box 6.

Buyer pays seller VAT-exclusive price of goods and enters VAT output tax in Box 2, VAT input tax in Box 4 and VAT exclusive price in Boxes 7 and 9.

Note that net amount of VAT due to HMRC is £Nil.

Buyer pays VAT-inclusive price to seller and makes no entries in VAT return because not registered.

Supply of services

Business to business (B2B) sales

Taxed in country of customer.

- If customer is outside EU, then no VAT.
  - Supplier includes net sale in Box 6.
- If customer is in EU then 'reverse charge' applies.
  - Customer treated as supplying goods to self
  - Customer treats as both a sale and a purchase
  - VAT (at local rate) included in Box 1 and 4, net cost included in Box 6 and 7
  - No VAT cost to customer provided they are not partially exempt
  - Supplier includes sale in Box 6.

Business to non-business (B2C) sales

The supplier charges VAT at the relevant local rate as they would do to a customer in the same country.

CBA focus

The European Union (EU) used to be known as the European Community (EC). Either term may be used in your assessment.

Overseas aspects of VAT are covered in the indirect tax reference material provided in the assessment in the 'Transaction outside the UK' section.

Completing the VAT return

The VAT account

- The main source of information for the VAT return.
- Must be maintained to show the amount due to (or from) HMRC at the end of each quarter.
- Figures extracted from the orginal business records (e.g. verified daybooks and journals).
- The balance on the VAT account should agree to the balance of VAT payable/ reclaimable on the VAT return.

In the assessment you may be asked to select a reason why the VAT account does not agree to the balance of VAT payable or repayable on the VAT return.

Information about the contents of a VAT account are included in the indirect tax reference material provided in the assessment in the 'Keeping business records and VAT records' section.

Pro-forma VAT account

1 April 20X5 to 30 June 20X5			
VAT deductible – input tax		**VAT payable – output tax**	
VAT charged on purchases	£p	VAT charged on sales	£p
April	X	April	X
May	X	May	X
June	X	June	X
VAT charged on imports	X		
VAT allowable on acquisitions from EU	X	VAT due on acquisitions from EU	X
Adjustments of previous errors			
(if within the error threshold – Chapter 5)			
Net input tax adjustments	X	Net output tax adjustments	X
Bad debt relief (see later)	X		
Less: VAT on credit notes received	(X)	Less: VAT on credit notes issued	(X)
	—		—
Total tax deductible	X	Total tax payable	X
	—	Less: Total tax deductible	(X)
			—
		Payable to HMRC	X
			—

Pro-forma VAT return

VAT due in the period on sales and other outputs (Box 1)	
VAT due in the period on acquisitions from other EU Member States (Box 2)	
Total VAT due (the sum of boxes 1 and 2) (Box 3)	
VAT reclaimed in the period on purchases and other inputs, including acquisitions from the EU (Box 4)	
Net VAT to be paid to HM Revenue & Customs or reclaimed (Difference between Boxes 3 and 4) (Box 5)	

Total value of sales and all other outputs excluding any VAT. Include your Box 8 figure (Box 6)	
	Whole pounds only
Total value of purchases and all other inputs excluding any VAT. Include your Box 9 figure (Box 7)	
	Whole pounds only
Total value of all supplies of goods and related costs, excluding any VAT, to other EU Member States (Box 8)	
	Whole pounds only
Total value of all acquisitions of goods and related costs, excluding any VAT, from other EU Member States (Box 9)	
	Whole pounds only

Boxes 3 and 5 are automatically completed online. However, practice questions will require you to complete these boxes yourself.

Information required for the VAT return

The following may all be used to complete the VAT return:

- VAT account
- Sales and sales returns ledger accounts
- Purchase and purchase returns ledger accounts
- Cash receipts and payment books
- Petty cash book
- Journal.

In addition you may be given information from the day books.

These ledgers must be prepared with

- integrity
- knowledge of requirements of VAT records and regulation of VAT administration.

Errors above the threshold (see Chapter 5)

- Cannot be entered on the VAT return
- Voluntary disclosure: inform the VAT office immediately either
  - by a letter or
  - on Form VAT 652.

CBA focus

Guidance on completing a VAT return is included in the indirect tax reference material provided in the assessment in the 'Completing the VAT return' section.

Relief for irrecoverable/ bad debts

```
                        ┌──────────────────────────┐
                        │  Relief for irrecoverable/│
                        │        bad debts          │
                        └──────────────────────────┘
```

Appears on VAT return as additional input tax. (Box 4)

Suppliers cannot issue credit notes to recover VAT on bad debts — must adjust through VAT returns.

If debt recovered at later date, must make adjustment to VAT relief claimed.

Reclaim VAT paid if:
- Output tax paid on original supply.
- Six months elapsed between:
  - date payment due, or date of supply, and
  - date of VAT return.
- Debt is less than 4 years and 6 months.
- Debt written off as bad debt in accounting records.

On the cessation of business:
- Can claim for all outstanding debts up to cessation.

On a takeover
- Can claim relief for target business bad debts if business bought as a going concern.

CBA focus

Details of VAT relief for irrecoverable/ bad debts is covered in the indirect reference material provided in the assessment, in the 'Bad debts' section.

CBA focus

As well as completing the VAT return in the assessment, you may be asked to draft or complete a short email.

It needs to be addressed to the relevant person, giving details of the return submission and the amount payable or receivable.

Index